Those were the days ...™

British
Lorries
of the 1960s

VELOCE

Other great books from Veloce –

Speedpro Series
4-cylinder Engine – How To Blueprint & Build A Short Block For High Performance (Hammill)
Alfa Romeo DOHC High-performance Manual (Kartalamakis)
Alfa Romeo V6 Engine High-performance Manual (Kartalamakis)
BMC 998cc A-series Engine – How To Power Tune (Hammill)
1275cc A-series High-performance Manual (Hammill)
Camshafts – How To Choose & Time Them For Maximum Power (Hammill)
Competition Car Datalogging Manual, The (Templeman)
Cylinder Heads – How To Build, Modify & Power Tune Updated & Revised Edition (Burgess & Gollan)
Distributor-type Ignition Systems – How To Build & Power Tune New 3rd Edition (Hammill)
Fast Road Car – How To Plan And Build Revised & Updated Colour New Edition (Stapleton)
Ford SOHC 'Pinto' & Sierra Cosworth DOHC Engines – How To Power Tune Updated & Enlarged Edition (Hammill)
Ford V8 – How To Power Tune Small Block Engines (Hammill)
Harley-Davidson Evolution Engines – How To Build & Power Tune (Hammill)
Holley Carburetors – How To Build & Power Tune Revised & Updated Edition (Hammill)
Honda Civic Type R, High-Performance Manual (Cowland & Clifford)
Jaguar XK Engines – How To Power Tune Revised & Updated Colour Edition (Hammill)
MG Midget & Austin-Healey Sprite – How To Power Tune New 3rd Edition (Stapleton)
MGB 4-cylinder Engine – How To Power Tune (Burgess)
MGB V8 Power – How To Give Your, Third Colour Edition (Williams)
MGB, MGC & MGB V8 – How To Improve New 2nd Edition (Williams)
Mini Engines – How To Power Tune On A Small Budget Colour Edition (Hammill)
Motorcycle-engined Racing Car – How To Build (Pashley)
Motorsport – Getting Started in (Collins)
Nissan GT-R High-performance Manual, The (Gorodji)
Nitrous Oxide High-performance Manual, The (Langfield)
Rover V8 Engines – How To Power Tune (Hammill)
Sportscar & Kitcar Suspension & Brakes – How To Build & Modify Revised 3rd Edition (Hammill)
SU Carburettor High-performance Manual (Hammill)
Successful Low-Cost Rally Car, How to Build a (Young)
Suzuki 4x4 – How To Modify For Serious Off-road Action (Richardson)
Tiger Avon Sportscar – How To Build Your Own Updated & Revised 2nd Edition (Dudley)
TR2, 3 & TR4 – How To Improve (Williams)
TR5, 250 & TR6 – How To Improve (Williams)
TR7 & TR8 – How To Improve (Williams)
V8 Engine – How To Build A Short Block For High Performance (Hammill)
Volkswagen Beetle Suspension, Brakes & Chassis – How To Modify For High Performance (Hale)
Volkswagen Bus Suspension, Brakes & Chassis – How To Modify For High Performance (Hale)
Weber DCOE, & Dellorto DHLA Carburetors – How To Build & Power Tune 3rd Edition (Hammill)

Those Were The Days ... Series
Alpine Trials & Rallies 1910-1973 (Pfundner)
American Trucks of the 1950s (Mort)
Anglo-American Cars From the 1930s to the 1970s (Mort)
Austerity Motoring (Bobbitt)
Austins, The last real (Peck)
Brighton National Speed Trials (Gardiner)
British Lorries Of The 1950s (Bobbitt)
British Lorries of the 1960s (Bobbitt)
British Touring Car Championship, The (Collins)
British Police Cars (Walker)
British Woodies (Peck)
Café Racer Phenomenon, The (Walker)
Dune Buggy Phenomenon (Hale)
Dune Buggy Phenomenon Volume 2 (Hale)
Hot Rod & Stock Car Racing in Britain In The 1980s (Neil)
Last Real Austins, The, 1946-1959 (Peck)
MG's Abingdon Factory (Moylan)
Motor Racing At Brands Hatch In The Seventies (Parker)
Motor Racing At Brands Hatch In The Eighties (Parker)
Motor Racing At Crystal Palace (Collins)
Motor Racing At Goodwood In The Sixties (Gardiner)
Motor Racing At Nassau In The 1950s & 1960s (O'Neil)
Motor Racing At Oulton Park In The 1960s (McFadyen)
Motor Racing At Oulton Park In The 1970s (McFadyen)
Superprix (Page & Collins)
Three Wheelers (Bobbitt)

Enthusiast's Restoration Manual Series
Citroën 2CV, How To Restore (Porter)
Classic Car Bodywork, How To Restore (Thaddeus)
Classic British Car Electrical Systems (Astley)
Classic Car Electrics (Thaddeus)
Classic Cars, How To Paint (Thaddeus)
Reliant Regal, How To Restore (Payne)
Triumph TR2, 3, 3A, 4 & 4A, How To Restore (Williams)
Triumph TR5/250 & 6, How To Restore (Williams)
Triumph TR7/8, How To Restore (Williams)
Volkswagen Beetle, How To Restore (Tyler)
VW Bay Window Bus (Paxton)
Yamaha FS1-E, How To Restore (Watts)

Essential Buyer's Guide Series
Alfa GT (Booker)
Alfa Romeo Spider Giulia (Booker & Talbott)
BMW GS (Henshaw)
BSA Bantam (Henshaw)
BSA Twins (Henshaw)
Citroën 2CV (Paxton)
Citroën ID & DS (Heilig)
Fiat 500 & 600 (Bobbitt)
Ford Capri (Paxton)
Jaguar E-type 3.8 & 4.2-litre (Crespin)
Jaguar E-type V12 5.3-litre (Crespin)
Jaguar XJ 1995-2003 (Crespin)
Jaguar/Daimler XJ6, XJ12 & Sovereign (Crespin)
Jaguar/Daimler XJ40 (Crespin)
Jaguar XJ-S (Crespin)
MGB & MGB GT (Williams)
Mercedes-Benz 280SL-560DSL Roadsters (Bass)
Mercedes-Benz 'Pagoda' 230SL, 250SL & 280SL Roadsters & Coupés (Bass)
Mini (Paxton)
Morris Minor & 1000 (Newell)
Porsche 928 (Hemmings)
Rolls-Royce Silver Shadow & Bentley T-Series (Bobbitt)
Subaru Impreza (Hobbs)
Triumph Bonneville (Henshaw)
Triumph Stag (Mort & Fox)
Triumph TR6 (Williams)
VW Beetle (Cservenka & Copping)
VW Bus (Cservenka & Copping)
VW Golf GTI (Cservenka & Copping)

Auto-Graphics Series
Fiat-based Abarths (Sparrow)
Jaguar MKI & II Saloons (Sparrow)
Lambretta Li Series Scooters (Sparrow)

Rally Giants Series
Audi Quattro (Robson)
Austin Healey 100-6 & 3000 (Robson)
Fiat 131 Abarth (Robson)
Ford Escort MkI (Robson)
Ford Escort RS Cosworth & World Rally Car (Robson)
Ford Escort RS1800 (Robson)
Lancia Stratos (Robson)
Mini Cooper/Mini Cooper S (Robson)
Peugeot 205 T16 (Robson)
Subaru Impreza (Robson)
Toyota Celica GT4 (Robson)

WSC Giants
Ferrari 312P & 312PB (Collins & McDonough)

General
1½-litre GP Racing 1961-1965 (Whitelock)
AC Two-litre Saloons & Buckland Sportscars (Archibald)
Alfa Romeo Giulia Coupé GT & GTA (Tipler)
Alfa Romeo Montreal – The dream car that came true (Taylor)
Alfa Romeo Montreal – The Essential Companion (Taylor)
Alfa Tipo 33 (McDonough & Collins)
Alpine & Renault – The Development Of The Revolutionary Turbo F1 Car 1968 to 1979 (Smith)
Anatomy Of The Works Minis (Moylan)
André Lefebvre, and the cars he created at Voisin and Citroën (Beck)
Armstrong-Siddeley (Smith)
Autodrome (Collins & Ireland)
Automotive A-Z, Lane's Dictionary Of Automotive Terms (Lane)
Automotive Mascots (Kay & Springate)
Bahamas Speed Weeks, The (O'Neil)
Bentley Continental, Corniche And Azure (Bennett)
Bentley MkVI, Rolls-Royce Silver Wraith, Dawn & Cloud/Bentley R & S-Series (Nutland)
BMC Competitions Department Secrets (Turner, Chambers & Browning)
BMW 5-Series (Cranswick)
BMW Z-Cars (Taylor)
BMW Boxer Twins 1970-1995 Bible, The (Falloon)
Britains Farm Model Balers & Combines 1967-2007, Pocket Guide to (Pullen)
Britains Farm Model & Toy Tractors 1998-2008, Pocket Guide to (Pullen)
British 250cc Racing Motorcycles (Pereira)
British Cars, The Complete Catalogue Of, 1895-1975 (Culshaw & Horrobin)
BRM – A Mechanic's Tale (Salmon)
BRM V16 (Ludvigsen)
BSA Bantam Bible, The (Henshaw)
Bugatti Type 40 (Price)
Bugatti 46/50 Updated Edition (Price & Arbey)
Bugatti T44 & T49 (Price & Arbey)
Bugatti 57 2nd Edition (Price)
Caravans, The Illustrated History 1919-1959 (Jenkinson)
Caravans, The Illustrated History From 1960 (Jenkinson)
Carrera Panamericana, La (Tipler)
Chrysler 300 – America's Most Powerful Car 2nd Edition (Ackerson)
Chrysler PT Cruiser (Ackerson)
Citroën DS (Bobbitt)
Classic British Car Electrical Systems (Astley)
Cliff Allison – From The Fells To Ferrari (Gauld)
Cobra – The Real Thing! (Legate)
Concept Cars, How to illustrate and design (Dewey)
Cortina – Ford's Bestseller (Robson)
Coventry Climax Racing Engines (Hammill)
Daimler SP250 New Edition (Long)
Datsun Fairlady Roadster To 280ZX – The Z-Car Story (Long)
Diecast Toy Cars of the 1950s & 1960s (Ralston)
Dino – The V6 Ferrari (Long)
Dodge Challenger & Plymouth Barracuda (Grist)
Dodge Charger – Enduring Thunder (Ackerson)
Dodge Dynamite! (Grist)
Donington (Boddy)
Draw & Paint Cars – How To (Gardiner)
Drive On The Wild Side, A – 20 Extreme Driving Adventures From Around The World (Weaver)
Ducati 750 Bible, The (Falloon)
Ducati 860, 900 And Mille Bible, The (Falloon)
Dune Buggy, Building A – The Essential Manual (Shakespeare)
Dune Buggy Files (Hale)
Dune Buggy Handbook (Hale)
Edward Turner: The Man Behind The Motorcycles (Clew)
Fast Ladies – Female Racing Drivers 1888 to 1970 (Bouzanquet)
Fiat & Abarth 124 Spider & Coupé (Tipler)
Fiat & Abarth 500 & 600 2nd Edition (Bobbitt)
Fiats, Great Small (Ward)
Fine Art Of The Motorcycle Engine, The (Peirce)
Ford F100/F150 Pick-up 1948-1996 (Ackerson)
Ford F150 Pick-up 1997-2005 (Ackerson)
Ford GT – Then, And Now (Streather)
Ford GT40 (Legate)
Ford In Miniature (Olson)
Ford Model Y (Roberts)
Ford Thunderbird From 1954, The Book Of The (Long)
Formula 5000 Motor Racing, Back then ... and back now (Lawson)
Forza Minardi! (Vigar)
Funky Mopeds (Skelton)
Gentleman Jack (Gauld)
GM In Miniature (Olson)
GT – The World's Best GT Cars 1953-73 (Dawson)
Hillclimbing & Sprinting – The Essential Manual (Short & Wilkinson)
Honda NSX (Long)
Intermeccanica - The Story of the Prancing Bull (McCredie & Reisner)
Jaguar, The Rise Of (Price)
Jaguar XJ-S (Long)
Jeep CJ (Ackerson)
Jeep Wrangler (Ackerson)
John Chatham - 'Mr Big Healey' – The Official Biography (Burr)
Karmann-Ghia Coupé & Convertible (Bobbitt)
Lamborghini Miura Bible, The (Sackey)
Lambretta Bible, The (Davies)
Lancia 037 (Collins)
Lancia Delta HF Integrale (Blaettel & Wagner)
Land Rover, The Half-ton Military (Cook)
Laverda Twins & Triples Bible 1968-1986 (Falloon)
Lea-Francis Story, The (Price)
Lexus Story, The (Long)
little book of smart, the New Edition (Jackson)
Lola – The Illustrated History (1957-1977) (Starkey)
Lola – All The Sports Racing & Single-seater Racing Cars 1978-1997 (Starkey)
Lola T70 – The Racing History & Individual Chassis Record 4th Edition (Starkey)
Lotus 49 (Oliver)
Marketingmobiles, The Wonderful Wacky World Of (Hale)
Mazda MX-5/Miata 1.6 Enthusiast's Workshop Manual (Grainger & Shoemark)
Mazda MX-5/Miata 1.8 Enthusiast's Workshop Manual (Grainger & Shoemark)
Mazda MX-5 Miata: The Book Of The World's Favourite Sportscar (Long)
Mazda MX-5 Miata Roadster (Long)
Maximum Mini (Booij)
MGA (Price Williams)
MGB & MGB GT– Expert Guide (Auto-doc Series) (Williams)
MGB Electrical Systems Updated & Revised Edition (Astley)
Micro Caravans (Jenkinson)
Micro Trucks (Mort)
Microcars At Large! (Quellin)
Mini Cooper – The Real Thing! (Tipler)
Mitsubishi Lancer Evo, The Road Car & WRC Story (Long)
Montlhéry, The Story Of The Paris Autodrome (Boddy)
Morgan Maverick (Lawrence)
Morris Minor, 60 Years On The Road (Newell)
Moto Guzzi Sport & Le Mans Bible, The (Falloon)
Motor Movies – The Posters! (Veysey)
Motor Racing – Reflections Of A Lost Era (Carter)
Motorcycle Apprentice (Cakebread)
Motorcycle Road & Racing Chassis Designs (Noakes)
Motorhomes, The Illustrated History (Jenkinson)
Motorsport In colour, 1950s (Wainwright)
Nissan 300ZX & 350Z – The Z-Car Story (Long)
Nissan GT-R Supercar: Born to race (Gorodji)
Off-Road Giants! – Heroes of 1960s Motorcycle Sport (Westlake)
Pass The Theory And Practical Driving Tests (Gibson & Hoole)
Peking To Paris 2007 (Young)
Plastic Toy Cars Of The 1950s & 1960s (Ralston)
Pontiac Firebird (Cranswick)
Porsche Boxster (Long)
Porsche 356 (2nd Edition) (Long)
Porsche 908 (Födisch, Neßhöver, Roßbach, Schwarz & Roßbach)
Porsche 911 Carrera – The Last Of The Evolution (Corlett)
Porsche 911R, RS & RSR, 4th Edition (Starkey)
Porsche 911 – The Definitive History 1963-1971 (Long)
Porsche 911 – The Definitive History 1971-1977 (Long)
Porsche 911 – The Definitive History 1977-1987 (Long)
Porsche 911 – The Definitive History 1987-1997 (Long)
Porsche 911 – The Definitive History 1997-2004 (Long)
Porsche 911SC 'Super Carrera' – The Essential Companion (Streather)
Porsche 914 & 914-6: The Definitive History Of The Road & Competition Cars (Long)
Porsche 924 (Long)
Porsche 928 (Long)
Porsche 944 (Long)
Porsche 964, 993 & 996 Data Plate Code Breaker (Streather)
Porsche 993 'King Of Porsche' – The Essential Companion (Streather)
Porsche 996 'Supreme Porsche' – The Essential Companion (Streather)
Porsche Racing Cars – 1953 To 1975 (Long)
Porsche Racing Cars – 1976 To 2005 (Long)
Porsche – The Rally Story (Meredith)
Porsche: Three Generations Of Genius (Meredith)
RAC Rally Action! (Gardiner)
Rallye Sport Fords: The Inside Story (Moreton)
Redman, Jim – 6 Times World Motorcycle Champion: The Autobiography (Redman)
Rolls-Royce Silver Shadow/Bentley T Series Corniche & Camargue Revised & Enlarged Edition (Bobbitt)
Rolls-Royce Silver Spirit, Silver Spur & Bentley Mulsanne 2nd Edition (Bobbitt)
Russian Motor Vehicles (Kelly)
RX-7 – Mazda's Rotary Engine Sportscar (Updated & Revised New Edition) (Long)
Scooters & Microcars, The A-Z Of Popular (Dan)
Scooter Lifestyle (Grainger)
Singer Story: Cars, Commercial Vehicles, Bicycles & Motorcycle (Atkinson)
SM – Citroën's Maserati-engined Supercar (Long & Claverol)
Speedway – Motor Racing's Ghost Tracks (Collins & Ireland)
Subaru Impreza: The Road Car And WRC Story (Long)
Supercar, How To Build your own (Thompson)
Tales from the Toolbox (Oliver)
Taxi! The Story Of The 'London' Taxicab (Bobbitt)
Tinplate Toy Cars Of The 1950s & 1960s (Ralston)
Toleman Story, The (Hilton)
Toyota Celica & Supra, The Book Of Toyota's Sports Coupés (Long)
Toyota MR2 Coupés & Spyders (Long)
Triumph Bonneville!, Save the – The inside story of the Meriden workers' co-op (Rosamond)
Triumph Motorcycles & The Meriden Factory (Hancox)
Triumph Speed Twin & Thunderbird Bible (Woolridge)
Triumph Tiger Cub Bible (Estall)
Triumph Trophy Bible (Woolridge)
Triumph TR6 (Kimberley)
Unraced (Collins)
Velocette Motorcycles – MSS To Thruxton Updated & Revised (Burris)
Virgil Exner – Visioneer: The Official Biography Of Virgil M Exner Designer Extraordinaire (Grist)
Volkswagen Bus Book, The (Bobbitt)
Volkswagen Bus Or Van To Camper, How To Convert (Porter)
Volkswagens Of The World (Glen)
VW Beetle Cabriolet (Bobbitt)
VW Beetle – The Car Of The 20th Century (Copping)
VW Bus – 40 Years Of Splitties, Bays & Wedges (Copping)
VW Bus Book, The (Bobbitt)
VW Golf: Five Generations Of Fun (Copping & Cservenka)
VW – The Air-cooled Era (Copping)
VW T5 Camper Conversion Manual (Porter)
VW Campers (Copping)
Works Minis, The Last (Purves & Brenchley)
Works Rally Mechanic (Moylan)

From Veloce Publishing's new imprints:

BATTLE CRY!

Soviet General & field rank officer uniforms: 1955 to 1991 (Streather)

Hubble & Hattie

My dog is blind – but lives life to the full! (Horsky)
Smellorama – nose games for your dog (Theby)
Waggy Tails & Wheelchairs (Epp)
Winston ... the dog who changed my life (Klute)

www.veloce.co.uk

First published in August 2009 by Veloce Publishing Limited, 33 Trinity Street, Dorchester DT1 1TT, England. Fax 01305 268864/e-mail info@veloce.co.uk/web www.veloce.co.uk or www.velocebooks.com.
ISBN: 978-1-84584-211-6/UPC: 6-36847-04211-0

Readers with ideas for automotive books, or books on other transport or related hobby subjects, are invited to write to the editorial director of Veloce Publishing at the above address.
British Library Cataloguing in Publication Data – A catalogue record for this book is available from the British Library. Typesetting, design and page make-up all by Veloce Publishing Ltd on Apple Mac. Printed in India by Replika Press.

Contents

Introduction and acknowledgements

'A wind of change,' the words of Prime Minister Harold Macmillan sum up the sixties as the decade of new horizons. Leaving the fifties behind, the country waved goodbye to an age of restrictions and austerity, and although 'Super Mac' was referring to South Africa when he made his Wind of Change speech, his terminology is nevertheless apt when used to describe Britain's commercial motor industry.

When the London Commercial Motor Show opened on 23rd September 1960, the 441 vehicles and trailers exhibited were almost exclusively of British manufacture. At the 1968 show, however, change was certainly the theme, and the representation of foreign vehicles indicated a turbulent future for Britain's lorry makers.

British lorries underwent enormous change during the sixties. Manufacturers such as Atkinson, ERF and Foden retained their traditional images until well into the decade, but the arrival of new-look cabs, revealing luxuries which previously would have been thought impossible, was nevertheless evident.

Revisions to the Construction and Use Regulations were, arguably, responsible for changes in vehicle design during the 1960s. The 'new look' began when Bedford introduced its TK range in the early years of the decade, its influence so monumental that it was only a matter of time before rival manufacturers were announcing new cab designs. Advancing technology meant the arrival of tilting cabs, twin-steer front axles, and larger, more powerful engines. In 1962, Britain remained the world's leading exporter of commercial vehicles, but times were a-changing ...

The outcome of amalgamating firms into large groups, a process which had begun in the fifties, materialised in the sixties when some familiar names were lost or fell foul to badge engineering. Thus, AEC, Albion, Austin, Commer, Dodge, Karrier, Leyland, Morris, Scammell and Thornycroft became merely badges owned by a few burgeoning combines.

More than anything else, lorry design and engineering in the sixties was influenced by Britain's, and Europe's, growing motorway network which, as well as affording easier and faster transportation, took long distance haulage into a new era.

Lorry owners and aficionados are a close-knit fraternity. Compiling this book has been an enjoyable, if daunting, experience, and I cannot help but feel an outsider looking in. Perhaps this adds an interesting, if curious, aspect to the following pages.

In preparing this volume I am grateful to those people who have allowed me to photograph their vehicles, and to Peter J. Davies and Michael Parker for permitting me to use their photographic material. My gratitude also goes to Commercial Motor, John Curwen and John Burrow, and to Andrew Minney, member of the Society of Automotive Historians and a motor industry researcher, for looking through my text and giving me the benefit of his expertise.

The majority of illustrations in this book are my own photographs from a collection of material garnered over many years. I have endeavoured to trace copyright holders where appropriate, but nevertheless offer my apologies if I have unknowingly offended in any respect.

Malcolm Bobbitt,
Cockermouth, Cumbria

'Rangeability with reliability' was Atkinson's message when it introduced its models for 1962. Seen here under the ownership of Peter McCallum & Sons of Aberdeen is the 150hp Gardner 6LX engine Atkinson eight-wheeler chassis and fibreglass all-vision de luxe cab, a favourite with fleets throughout Britain. (Author's collection)

Lorries from past eras are valued by haulage companies as ideal publicity vehicles. Many hauliers , such as Wm Halliday with his 1969 Foden, are keen classic vehicle enthusiasts who hold on to their older workhorses for posterity and enjoy showing them at commercial vehicle events. (Author's collection)

The swinging sixties

As the fifties ended, a new motoring age dawned with Britain about to take a political leap by joining the European Common Market.

Leaving behind an era dominated by austerity, and with growing prosperity giving a welcome 'feel-good' factor, the prospect of change was to produce a measure of uncertainty which ultimately had a significant effect on Britain's commercial vehicle industry. Moreover, the country's embryonic motorway network was affording rapid inter-city travel at a time when a shrinking railway system meant that increasing tonnages of freight were being transferred to road transport.

Joining the Common Market would provide greater opportunities in trading, which, in turn, promised to affect lorry design if hauliers were to travel longer distances with ever-increasing payloads. It would also mean that foreign lorry makers would expand their markets by giving willing British customers greater choice when it came to buying vehicles.

During the sixties, evolving technology meant that vehicle manufacturers were able to unveil new chassis designs as well as offer cabs that were, compared to previous types, quite lavish in respect of comfort, ergonomics, sound-proofing and trim materials. No more would drivers have to suffer the vagaries of climate, instead they could enjoy car-like conditions in terms of seating, heating and ventilation.

The 'new' lorry on the street in the early sixties was the Thames Trader, which was announced in 1957. Its modern looks (the vehicle depicted is a Mk II) are a contrast to the Albion and Leyland seen at a Westmorland auction, and note the more modern KM and TK Bedfords. (Author's collection)

British Lorries of the 1960s

The Thames Trader was the modern look for Ford whose vehicles had, until the late fifties and early sixties, pretty well portrayed 1940s styling. Appearance wasn't everything, however, as under the skin Ford relied upon well-tried technology, and drivers liked the vehicle and its cab layout. (Author's collection)

Pictured in Scotland in 2008, Robert Johnstone & Son's Thames Trader is seen in company with the firm's Albion Chieftain II, which is parked adjacent to an AEC. In the distance is a 1950s AEC. Both Albion and AEC became absorbed under the Leyland umbrella in 1951 and 1962 respectively. (Author's collection)

Thames Traders were put to a variety of uses, not least as recovery vehicles. In service with C&W Ellis of Kendal, this Ford was pictured at Kirkby Stephen one Easter weekend when it was on hand to give help to stricken vehicles participating in the annual lorry run which takes place in steep hills on isolated roads. (Author's collection)

From this brochure detail of the 1957 Thames Trader it is possible to see, looking at the previous images, the result of styling modifications made to the model range over the seven-year period. Initially built to cater for payloads of between 30cwt and 3 tons, lorries of 4, 5 and 7 tons eventually became available. (Author's collection)

In addition to forward-control Traders, Ford produced the NC range of bonneted vehicles. Though mechanical components were largely interchangeable with the forward-control vehicles, wheelbase dimensions differed considerably. This example is owned by E.M. Eyels & Son of North Yorkshire. (Author's collection)

You get a

TOUCH

OF

GENIUS

in everything

made by

ROOTES

KARRIER 'BANTAM' 2-3 TONNER
Well proportioned and exceptionally manoeuvrable, this quality-built low-loading truck with superb wide-vision cab is available with either petrol or diesel engine. In tractor-trailer form it handles a 4-5 ton pay load.

COMMER 7 TON FORWARD CONTROL DROPSIDER For toughness and reliability this amply-powered forward control dropsider will take a lot of beating. Available with petrol or Rootes diesel engine, and choice of two wheelbases.

COMMER 'SUPERPOISE' 5 TON TIPPER Ideal for heavy duty work, this robust petrol or diesel powered vehicle has an all-steel 5 cu.yd. dropsider body built to withstand the roughest usage. A typical example of Commer quality.

The Rootes catalogue, published to coincide with the 1960 Commercial Motor Show, shows the lightweight 2/3-tonner Karrier Bantam. Continuing the forward-control theme is the Commer 7-ton, while the mid-range conventional lorry is Commer's Superpoise 5-tonner.

For Rootes, the early sixties was a time of unrest. Strikes within the motor industry, and particularly at British Light Steel Pressings, meant that supplies of panels for the Karrier Bantam were jeopardized. Rootes management chose not to enter into agreement with the strikers and ultimately the cost to the company in lost production, sales and profit was enormous. Revealing a £2m loss in 1962, Rootes sold a significant portion of its shareholding to Chrysler. (Courtesy Rootes publicity/author's collection)

Ford produced some high quality publicity material; here it depicts the larger payload Thames Trader at work. Customers could opt for 4888cc petrol or 5416cc diesel engines, but, even at early sixties fuel prices, the petrol version would have been expensive to run compared to the oil burner. (Courtesy Ford publicity material/author's collection)

During the 1960s there was a gradual re-branding of the Austin and Morris marques to BMC, and badge engineering was as popular in the commercial vehicle sector as it was in the car market. Note the different grilles used for Austin, i.e. two horizontal bars as opposed to four for the 1963 Morris range, then Austin's change to the Morris profile. Vehicles could be supplied with different body formats to include trucks, tippers and rigid styles, as well as special-purpose types to include tankers, concrete transporters, refuse collectors and horseboxes. In the forward-control range of vehicles depicted, engine configurations were 4-litre petrol and 5.1- and 5.7-litre diesels, according to model type. Four-speed gearboxes were specified as standard, but five-speed ones were optional, according to model. (Author's collection)

New for the early sixties from Morris was the FG series, which could be specified with either a 2.2-litre petrol or diesel engine. Morris advertising referred to this series of trucks as being 'Angled Planned'; the example pictured here was seen at a garage on a snowy day. (Author's collection)

When BMC's Austin-badged 702 appeared at the end of the 1950s it was largely a restyled 701. During the 1960s some styling and engineering modifications were introduced; the position of the indicators for example, which, rather than being below the headlights, mirrored the FH range of vehicles. Wearing Castrol decals and trade plates, this Austin was probably

Scammell's Townsman three-wheeler was introduced in 1964 to replace the Scarab. Orders for the new model, with its fibreglass cab, were mainly received from British Railways and the GPO, though some smaller organisations specified it for marshalling duties. (Courtesy Scammell/Gregg Coyner & Co/author's collection)

This preserved Scammell Townsman portrays the vehicle's fussy appearance, accentuated by the positioning of the headlights and the dodgem car-like bumper. Just visible is the air intake built into the cab roof above the windscreen and below the registration plate, cooling air being carried by trunking down the cab rear panel to the radiator. Reliant built the cabs for early Townsmans; Thornycroft supplied the later examples. (Author's collection)

Though the Scammell Townsman entered production in 1964, Scarabs remained available until 1967, the example here wearing a 1966 registration. Known as mechanical horses, these vehicles are a favourite with commercial vehicle enthusiasts. (Author's collection)

Bigger and different to the Townsman, though smaller than the typical Scammell, the Handyman made its debut in 1960, the model here being the 1963 Handyman 2. The vehicle was for sale when photographed in 2008, its owner claiming it to be one of only two in existence. When introduced, the Handyman was specified with a choice of Gardner 112 or 150bhp engines or Leyland's 125 or 150bhp units. The gearbox was Scammell's six-speed overdrive-top, unit-mounted with the engine to reduce vehicle length. The two-piece plastic cab is distinctive in appearance and, at the time of its launch at the London Commercial Motor Show, offered good driving conditions. At its debut the Handyman four-wheel tractor unit, with its 8ft 6½in wheelbase, was described as basically a forward-control version of the bonneted Highwayman. (Author's collection)

For the 1960s, ERF decided to give its vehicles a more modern appearance and introduced twin headlights, while retaining the familiar split-screen cab. The firm's tractor units came in a variety of wheelbase lengths according to engine specification, Gardner being used exclusively. The tractor unit depicted was photographed on a wet afternoon in 2008. (Author's collection)

ERFs of the fifties and sixties were easily identified because of their distinctive frontal designs; the twin headlights signify this Gardner diesel-engined vehicle to be from the early part of the latter decade. At this time ERFs were fitted with disc brakes, the first commercial vehicle manufacturer to fit them to a standard chassis. (Author's collection)

Cabs for ERFs, such as this 1964 example belonging to R.J. Rich & Son of Longridge in Lancashire, were built by Jennings & Sons Ltd of Sandbach, Cheshire, which is the home of ERF and Foden. Jennings had supplied cabs to ERF since the 1930s, the coachbuilder eventually being incorporated within the company. (Author's collection)

Bedford's JO ½-ton pick-up was designed for smaller payloads and, combining lorry-like principles with car-engined technology, used the 2651cc Vauxhall engine fitted to the PASX/PADX Velox/Cresta saloons. Though its performance was more than adequate, the JO did not sell in huge numbers. (Author's collection)

The TK was introduced at the 1960 Commercial Motor Show and was Bedford's success story of the decade. The vehicle set new standards in cab design and comfort, which helped make it a bestseller, while technical details, such as having payloads from 3-ton rigids to 12-ton tractor units, made it suitable for most purposes. One of the first fleets to specify was Foster Clark's, the firm renowned for custard and other foods. (Courtesy Bedford/author's collection)

Bedford's TK range included diesel-engined tractor units designed for deliveries in urban areas and confined spaces. The 4- and 5-ton tractor units had 84in (213cm) wheelbases for excellent manoeuvrability. (Courtesy Bedford/author's collection)

This 1962 Bedford TK has pride of place in J.R. Breward & Sons' (haulage contractors of Bishops Auckland, County Durham) fleet of vehicles, and was pictured in 2004. TK production began late in the summer of 1960, and it became one of the most familiar lorries on British roads during the sixties and seventies. (Author's collection)

Much more successful than the JO was Bedford's larger and more powerful TJ. Smaller payload TJs up to 4 tons had 'eyebrows' and vertical grille slats, as seen on this vehicle pictured alongside a 'modern' ERF. (Author's collection)

Bedford TJs over 4 tons had horizontal grille slats and were without the hooded headlight cowls. Looking resplendent and owned by a builder's merchant, this restored 1967 TJ was pictured in 2007, the door decals reading Bodge & Scarna!

Badge engineering was a feature of the sixties, and is exemplified in this and the following picture. For 1960, Scammell – which had been under Leyland control since 1955 – brought out the forward-control Trunker 10-wheeler powered by a Gardner 6LX engine mated to a six-speed (Scammell) gearbox. (Courtesy Scammell advertising/author's collection)

Apart from minor styling detail, the cab employed on this 1966-registered Albion (the Scottish lorry builder having been incorporated within the Leyland empire in 1951) is the same as that fitted to the previously seen Scammell. On the right is a 1972/3-registered ERF-hauled Castrol tanker. (Author's collection)

The heavy mob: a 1965-registered Scammell Highwayman is seen passing a heavy haulage breakdown truck (in this instance an Albion) at a busy vintage event in July 2002. These really were the prime movers of the sixties, often seen on Britain's roads. (Author's collection)

For the new decade, Austin's conventional vehicle layout, rather than forward-control, is showing its ancestry, despite the one-piece windscreen, twin headlights and modernised grille. Pictured in May 2006 at Carlisle airport, and having a 1964 Dumfriesshire registration, the vehicle is well-presented and representative of a design that, at one time, was very familiar. (Author's collection)

Austin's FFK100 series forward-control lorries performed as general workhorses, this 1964 example is pictured whilst in service with E.A. Hughes of Bewdley in Worcestershire. Customers could choose between a 4-litre petrol engine or 5.1-litre diesel; four-speed transmission was standard with five-speeds being optional, along with a range of chassis configurations.

Superb driver comfort was the marketing message when Commer introduced its CA 10-, 11- and 12-ton forward-control tractor range in 1962. The CA was inspired by Bedford's TK series, and was fitted with the Tilling-Stevens TS-3 engine coupled to a five-speed constant-mesh gearbox. The TS-3 was a two-stroke, three-cylinder opposed-piston diesel engine which was novel as far as the commercial vehicle industry was concerned, though its development can be traced back to 1948. (Author's collection)

Atkinsons of Walton-Le-Dale in Lancashire are amongst the best known commercial vehicles in the world. This 1964 rigid eight-wheeler Castrol tanker with trailer made for a powerful picture when photographed in 2006. The twin headlights give the cab a modern appearance despite the split windscreen which gives it character. (Author's collection)

Carrying the load

Hauliers and transport companies in the sixties, conveying everything from food produce to household goods as well as specialist materials to keep the wheels of industry turning, were facing challenges in many areas of operation.

Motorways resulted in quicker turnarounds while, at the same time, the higher levels of road traffic lead to increasing restrictions and difficulties in loading and effecting deliveries.

New technology, such as the advent of container traffic, heralded changing practices in deliveries to and from docks. This, and the arrival of the roadrailing scheme, meant that hauliers were often forced to invest in expensive equipment, without which they would have been unable to survive in business. In some instances, use of rigid lorries gave way to articulated types in order that tractor units could shuttle between jobs with greater operating flexibility.

Permitted payloads were increasing, and to take advantage of new legislation both manufacturer and haulier had little choice but to adapt to new practices. If they didn't, others would. Chassis design underwent change, and, as a result, modifications and innovations in respect of suspension, tyres, braking and transmission, not to mention more powerful engines, came about. Then there was the question of running costs, and the effort to keep these as low as possible whilst maintaining vehicle and component reliability. A vehicle off the road was a vehicle not earning its keep.

Not a pretty sight! Pictured in 2006, this well-used 1960s Atkinson is dilapidated but, nevertheless, in working order and generating power for a country show amusements site. (Author's collection)

By 1960s standards, Albion's Claymore wasn't exactly at the cutting edge of styling but was, however, as technically advanced as other lorries of its time. Power was derived from Albion's own 4.1-litre horizontal diesel engine positioned beneath the cab. (Author's collection)

This 1966-registered Albion Claymore is seen with its wartime Morris Commercial cargo. Claymores were built as 4- and 5-tonners, the 4.1-litre diesel coupled to either five- or six-speed gearboxes. A choice of 10ft (304.8cm), 11ft 10in (360.7cm) or 12ft 10in (391.2cm) wheelbases were available to suit body lengths of up to 18ft (548.6cm). (Author's collection)

'Maids of all work' is one way of describing Fodens such as this 1967-registered lorry. Some examples from this era had twin horizontal headlights in a nacelle, others the arrangement seen here. (Author's collection)

In 1966, Jack Bradley of Accrington purchased a number of International Motor trucks from the distributor R. Cripps of Nottingham. Experience with Internationals showed them to have exceptional fuel economy compared with other vehicles. Internationals were built at Doncaster in England between 1965 and 1969, and were based on the American Paystar range which, for the UK market, was known as Loadstar. (Courtesy Cripps/IH/Jack Bradley publicity/author's collection)

Wearing Jack Bradley of Accrington decals, this International Loadstar was photographed in 2002. It could well be one of the lorries seen in the accompanying publicity item. (Author's collection)

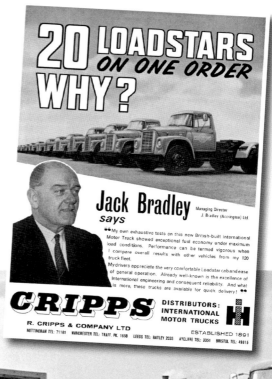

These mainly 1960s ERFs were pictured at a vintage event in 2007. Note the differing cab styles, the lorry third from left dating from 1959. (Author's collection)

Compare the above photograph with this publicity image showing W. Davey & Co Ltd's twin-steer ERF when new. Gardner engines were specified, as were air-assisted braking and five-speed gearboxes. (Courtesy D. Cook)

Thornycroft retained its reputation as a supplier of well-engineered specialist vehicles after being acquired by AEC in 1961, when this Mastiff MH in service with Merralls Transport of Egham was pictured with its consignment of drums. The MH six-wheeler introduced in 1960 had a 20-ton gross payload. (Courtesy Peter Davies)

Seen wearing the livery of Cameron's Brewery Company, this Foden is particularly stylish with its headlights faired into the front wheelarches. Vehicles as resplendent as this are revered amongst lorry enthusiasts. Surely it is no coincidence that the licence plate letters of this vehicle spell ALE? (Author's collection)

This colourful advertisement appeared to coincide with the 1960 Commercial Motor Show, and depicts Foden's FE6/24 eight-wheeler in service with Fraser Bros of Greenock. It is no coincidence that the freighter moored in the harbour is equipped with a Foden 150bhp 2-stroke oil engine, the same as that powering the lorry, to drive the vessel's 60kW generator which in turn supplies power to the steering, derricks, lighting and heating. (Courtesy Foden publicity/author's collection)

BMC's 'planned comfort' cab had step rings on the front wheels, grab handles and a reinforced intermediate step; door trims are of durable vinyl-treated fabric. (Courtesy BMC/author's collection)

Cab styling as seen here was adopted by Foden when it introduced its tilting cab in 1962, the first British lorry builder to offer such a design for quantity production. A feature of American cabs for some time, British manufacturers had not developed the tilting cab on grounds of increased cost as well as weight. (Author's collection)

Arlington was a major coachbuilder and supplier of commercial vehicles with branches throughout the Home Counties. An AEC, a Bedford and an Albion, the latter by then under Leyland ownership, are seen at a publicity event. The Albion is wearing Royale Prams livery, the Bedford has Mace Marketing/Wm Evans & Co decals, and the AEC is operated by J&H (Peckham) Transport Services Ltd. (Courtesy Artricia Industrial Pictures/author's collection)

By the early sixties, badge engineering had caught up with Albion and Leyland, the former in Chieftain guise seen here with its four-cylinder engine and choice of five- or six-speed gearbox. The larger 10-ton Reiver was built as a six-wheeler, the 12-ton Chieftain-Scammell as a tractor chassis, and the 9-ton Clydesdale as a 125hp six-cylinder designed for heavy duty. (Author's collection)

The face of Leyland in the early sixties displaying the corporate image shared with Albion. The Leyland range comprised the standard diesel-engined 2.26-litre 2-tonner, 12-ton Comet and 12/14-ton Super-Comet, 12-ton Beaver (as depicted), 48-ton Hippo and 140hp lightweight eight-wheeler Octopus. Cab design was influenced by stylist Michelotti. (Author's collection)

At the time of the 1962 Commercial Motor Show, AEC had acquired Thornycroft and was merging with Leyland. AEC publicity material was particularly evocative, showing here the bulk transport 24-ton Mammoth Major and the 12/14-ton Mercury which, when articulated, increased to 18/24 tons. The differences between the two cabs are minimal, the Mammoth Major having a split windscreen whilst the Mercury had a single piece affair.

The amalgamation of Leyland with AEC, itself part of Associated Commercial Vehicles (ACV), was a protracted affair, negotiations having been on and off since the mid-1950s. In 1960 there had been a possibility of BMC taking over ACV, but in the event it was talks between Donald Stokes and Henry Spurrier of Leyland, and Lord Brabazon and Sir William Black of ACV which led to the acquisition of ACV (and AEC) by Leyland in 1962. (Author's collection)

MAMMOTH MAJOR

Built for bulk transport—the 24 ton gross
MAMMOTH MAJOR 8. Three wheelbases, 14 ft. 8 in. to 17 ft. 4¼ in.;
140 or 192 b.h.p. engines: numerous specification variations.

MERCURY

Adaptability for every type of load—
the MERCURY 12 and 14 tons gross solo, 18 and 24 tons articulated. Seven wheelbases,
economy 130 b.h.p. engine, wide spread of gear ratios, vacuum or air brakes.

SOUTHALL · MIDDLESEX

Though it carries a 1970/71 registration, the Atkinson nearest the camera very much illustrates its sixties origins, particularly in the split windscreen, at a time when some of the manufacturer's other vehicles were displaying new cab styles.
(Author's collection)

An intrinsic aspect of moving freight in the 1960s was the Roadrailer made by the Pressed Steel Company at Linwood in Scotland. This door-to-door road/rail freight carrier could be interchanged between rail and road usage in a claimed 90 seconds so that it could be used, with a tractor unit, as a road vehicle or, with rail wheels in place, as part of a freight train.
(Author's collection)

(Opposite, bottom left) By the early '60s motorway travel had become common, but views with sparse traffic like this were to be shortlived, especially as companies began to transfer from rail freight to road. The vehicle is a Kew-built Dodge which had payload ratings from 5 to 9 tons and choice of wheelbase lengths. (Courtesy Dodge publicity item/author's collection)

Correctly loading a lorry so that its cargo remains safe is vitally important. One wonders whether this consignment of oil drums, seen on a Thames Trader in the early sixties, would be acceptable today ... The drums loaded lengthwise look as if they are tied down securely, but that doesn't mean they wouldn't shift in the event of the vehicle braking heavily or swerving. (Courtesy India Tyres publicity item/author's collection)

Scenes like this were an everyday sight on Britain's roads in the sixties. The Thames Trader with its over-cab box-type body looks as if it is holding up the traffic, which includes a Leyland Comet. (Courtesy India Tyres publicity item/author's collection)

Atkinson's Weightmaster series of vehicles was marketed to operate at a maximum of 14 tons (Weightmaster Four), 18 tons (Weightmaster Six), and the 24-ton Weightmaster Eight as pictured here. All were fitted with two-speed axles and five-speed gearboxes. (Courtesy Atkinson vehicles/author's collection)

Another view of Aberdeen haulage contractor Peter McCallum's 1964 Atkinson serves as a reminder that such vehicles were a familiar sight on Britain's trunk roads, the A1 and A9 providing a continuous route between London and the north of Scotland. Britain's expanding motorway network enabled hauliers to reduce travel times and maximise pick-up and drop-off schedules. (Author's collection)

This is the face of Atkinson in 1968, the lorry maker choosing to retain the split windscreen cab configuration. Improvements to cab design meant it was wider than previous types and had greater driver comfort. (Courtesy Atkinson publicity/author's collection)

Hoveringham Gravel Ltd's tipper featured as part of Foden's advertising in the early to mid-sixties. The claimed performance from the 175bhp vehicle with its maximum payload of 17 tons was 10.20mpg fully laden, which also allowed for 50mph easy motorway cruising. The move from rail to road freight in the mid-sixties was largely the result of the contraction of railway activities, i.e. Beeching's rationalisation of rail freight services. (Courtesy Foden publicity/author's collection)

Foden lorries of the late 1960s retained a measure of corporate styling left over from earlier designs, but were modern nonetheless, with their full-width one-piece windscreen cabs based on structures supplied by Motor Panels Ltd. Vehicles, such as the type seen here, were powered by Gardner diesel engines and Foden 12-speed gearboxes, but some had 200bhp Leyland engines coupled to 10-speed semi-automatic gearboxes. (Author's collection)

Albion introduced its 'ergomatic' cab, which had previously been announced for the AEC and Leyland ranges but with lighter gauge panelling and dedicated badging, in 1966. This is the Super Reiver 20 six-wheeler approved for operation at 20 tons gross, and could be specified with a long wheelbase chassis, double drive and lockable third differential.
(Courtesy Albion publicity/author's collection)

Jack Bradley's British-built Internationals have been detailed elsewhere in the book, but two examples of this rarity together surely warrants another mention. Next to the already seen SWW 410F is a 1966 version of this American-designed lorry produced over a four-year period at Doncaster in the 1960s. (Author's collection)

Though strictly outside the remit of this book, the Commando was the last Commer lorry to be built. Development began in 1968, and by the end of 1969 a number of prototypes were undergoing testing in advance of a February 1974 launch. This 1975 example was pictured in November 2002, delivering potatoes. (Author's collection)

Pulling power

Heavy haulage evokes a number of scenes; conventional lorries, fully laden, en route to a delivery, as well as leviathans in charge of abnormal loads, crawling along the highway with little more velocity than a snail.

All the mainstream lorry manufacturers catered for the heavy haulage market. The badges of AECs, Atkinsons, Bedfords, Commers, ERFs, Fodens, Guys and Leylands were familiar sights on Britain's trunk roads and motorways. The two big names in heavy haulage were Scammell and Thornycroft; these one-time independent concerns ultimately being absorbed, by convoluted routes, under the Leyland umbrella.

Today, abnormal loads are transported by motorway for much of their journey. In the 1960s, however, when the network was fragmented but nevertheless expanding, this was not always possible. Towns, cities and villages were obstacles on expeditions which had to be carefully negotiated to take account of the sharpest bends, steepest hills, lowest bridges and narrowest roads. Journeys sometimes took several days to complete, and needed police escorts throughout.

A feature of the London Commercial Motor Shows, which were held biennially, was the increasing appearance of foreign lorries in the heavy haulage category to rival the prime movers in Britain's haulage industry. Conversely, British makes such as Atkinson, Foden, Scammell and Thornycroft were satisfying overseas markets.

The expertise of Britain's premier heavy haulage firms was, and still is, revered worldwide. If the British couldn't undertake a particular task, the chances were nobody could.

Few lorries are bigger than AEC's Militant, which was used for military as well as civilian purposes. A one-time army vehicle, the 1969 colossus pictured here is now in the hands of a collector, and was photographed in 2005. (Author's collection)

Breakdown trucks capable of rescuing heavy lorries were often seen at garages along Britain's trunk roads. The type of Commer pictured here at a vintage vehicle event was introduced in 1962, the heaviest of which was marketed as the 20/22-ton gross Maxiload. By 1964, Rootes was in talks with Chrysler regarding the American giant acquiring part of the British company, and in 1967, owing to Rootes' financial position, there was a full takeover. (Author's collection)

COMMER four-wheel drive
CROSS-COUNTRY MODELS
Maximum Gross Vehicle Weight 18,000 lb. (8,150 kg)

ROOTES PRODUCTS — BUILT STRONGER TO LAST LONGER!

Heavy haulage and cross-country work was the domain of Commer's four-wheel drive models which were designed and built in conjunction with All-Wheel Drives Ltd. Two versions were available, Commer petrol and Perkins diesel, 4750cc and 5800cc respectively, with two wheelbase lengths, 12ft (3.657m) and 14ft 1in (4.292m). (Commer publicity/author's collection)

All-terrain Commers had chassis of orthodox construction that were reinforced where necessary to meet the demands of the vehicle's off-road operation. Transmission comprised a four-speed gearbox with transfer box and additional sliding spur gear for the option of rear- or all-wheel drive, and to cope with exceptionally severe gradients. (Commer publicity/author's collection)

Commer's cross-country vehicle was designed with a cab similar to the one specified for the firm's Superpoise models, and was acclaimed for its roominess, comfort, use of controls and ability to withstand the roughest conditions. (Commer publicity/author's collection)

This is the face of Seddon in the mid-1960s, before the company took over its rival, Atkinson. Contemporary advertising claimed the 13:four, priced at £1710, to be affordable by any contractor in the country. Specification included the brand new 'Supa-cab,' Perkins 354 120bhp engine and full air braking. (Author's collection)

Heavy-haulage, Albion style, in pouring rain during the 2005 Easter weekend. Registered in 1959, the 1957 model Albion, owned by Walkers of Greenock, was in service throughout the sixties and seventies. (Author's collection)

GREAT NEW RANGE FROM GUY 'BIG J'

'Great new range from Guy.' The 'Big J' was an obvious reference to Jaguar which bought Guy in the early sixties. This publicity item, depicting a Guy being overtaken by an E-type Jaguar, is emotive to say the least. Before Jaguar's purchase of Guy in 1961, the lorry maker had embarked upon a new look with its fibreglass cabs. When Jaguar became part of BMH in 1964, the 'Big J' range reverted to steel cabs. (Author's collection)

Scammell's Handyman of the late 1960s was originally designed for British Road Services, but was adopted for general sale. Fitted with a Leyland 0.680 engine and an AEC six-speed gearbox, this vehicle was photographed in 2003, the centre of attention as the driver attempts to reverse into a space. (Author's collection)

This evocative publicity artwork exemplifies the type of heavy haulage associated with the building and construction industries. The Perkins diesel-engined V-series Commers are identified by the Sankey-built cabs that have two horizontal slats and single headlamps. (Commer publicity/author's collection)

Foden was a major player when it came to serving the construction industry, and designed a half-cab for special use vehicles. With its outward-sloping windscreen, the cab was exceptionally roomy and fully insulated for sound and temperature. The rear wheels of this cement mixer are of the single type to afford as much traction as possible when working on building sites. (Courtesy Foden/author's collection)

For heavy transport, Foden introduced this 32-ton tractor unit with container trailer in 1968. The cab design is unusual, and is a full-width alternative to that seen on the vehicle pictured on the opposite page. The engine is a 210bhp Gardner mated to a Foden twelve-speed gearbox. (Courtesy Foden/author's collection)

Looking to the future when legal requirements and export orders permitted, Foden introduced this 44-ton gross chassis at the 1968 Commercial Motor Show. Specification includes a 275bhp engine, twelve-speed gearbox, 32-ton rear bogie and a hydraulically-mounted all-metal saloon cab with a forward-sloping windscreen that was designed to prevent dazzle. (Courtesy Foden/author's collection)

A more conventional-looking Foden is seen here in this heavily retouched publicity photograph depicting a typical Thames-side coal wharf serving London's power stations, Battersea being visible across the river. Foden eight-wheelers were the mainstay of many heavy haulage fleets. (Courtesy Foden/author's collection)

Redundant military vehicles like this AEC often found their way to heavy haulage operators and were used as recovery vehicles. On England's Pennine routes such as the A59, A6, A65, A66 and A69, rescuing stricken heavy lorries was a specialist task. (Author's collection)

Atkinson's Viewline
was the only cab of
entirely new design at
the 1966 Commercial
Motor Show. Affording
maximum visibility,
with its short axle-
to-bumper distance
the cab set new
standards in visibility,
driver comfort and
maintenance. The
Viewline was originally
specified with a
Cummins 240bhp diesel
engine and ten-speed
David Brown gearbox.

Atkinson models
introduced at the 1968
Commercial Motor show
were the Borderer,
Searcher, Defender and
Leader. The lorry maker
had also produced a
number of vehicles for
Pickfords, the 1968
Omega being the last
bonneted type built
for that firm. Atkinson
was later bought
by Seddon Diesels
Vehicles Ltd, which in
turn was acquired by
International Harvester.
(Author's collection)

Under the auspices of Leyland Motors, in the late 1960s
BMC introduced its range of Mastiff vehicles comprising
16-ton rigid and 24/26-ton tractor units combined with the
'Pilot' cab. Power was derived from a compact 8.3-litre V8
located under the cab floor. (Author's collection)

The chassis design of the Mastiff tractor unit was configured from that of an existing BMC/Leyland vehicle to comprise a hefty deep U-section arrangement for heavy haulage operation. (Author's collection)

The Pilot tilt cab of BMC's Mastiff was comprehensively equipped with a fully adjustable driver's seat upholstered in a breathable black Ambla material. The contemporary brochure mentions the cab as having a car-style layout, rubber carpeting, padded facia and full instrumentation. (Author's collection)

(Below) Thornycroft's Mighty Antar was the biggest tractor unit built in Britain. With a Rolls-Royce C8CSFL eight-cylinder 16.2-litre engine, it was an essential part of the army's tank transport fleet, the in-line engine design being favoured over the V8s as supplied to other customers. The dimensions of the in-line engine compared to those of the V8 called for a longer bonnet than would otherwise be fitted. (Courtesy Thornycroft/author's collection)

Scammell's expertise made it a specialist company. Such was its professionalism that it was able to design and build vehicles to meet specific tasks. For off-road work the Constructor, with its bogie articulation, had few rivals, and here a recovery vehicle is rescuing another Scammell in a contrived publicity image. (Courtesy Scammell/author's collection)

SCAMMELL CONTRACTOR
GIANT OF ROADS, GIANT OF THE SHOW!

SEE IT ON STAND 79

Scammell is synonymous with heavy haulage, and the Contractor, which replaced the Constructor for operations of up to 240 tons gross, was highly successful in undertaking varied applications. One of the biggest vehicles on show at the 1966 Commercial Motor Show, the Contractor 6x4 – with its Cummins NH250 240bhp engine and semi-automatic eight-speed gearbox – was the centre of attention. Whether the Contractor has the visual appeal of its predecessor is a matter of opinion! (Author's collection)

Amongst the best-known heavy hauliers are Wynns and Pickfords. The latter is depicted in this instance with a 6x6 Scammell Constructor, designed for drawbar trailer work, in charge of a consignment of 250-ton gross trailer weight. (Courtesy Scammell/author's collection)

Scammells were employed by the army for tank transporter work, tractor units being specified with a choice of three six-cylinder engines; Leyland's O/680 four-stroke diesel of 161bhp at 2000rpm, Rolls-Royce's C6NFL 200bhp at 2200rpm four-stroke diesel, or Cummins' 212bhp NH220. (Courtesy Scammell/author's collection)

The preserve of the fairground fraternity was the Scammell Highwayman, this Gardner-engined vehicle dating from 1967. When the vehicle pictured here was built, Scammell, having been under Leyland control for twelve years, had been allowed to continue in much the same way as it had done for generations. Things were about to change, however, as Leyland exercised greater control over this unique firm. (Author's collection)

The export scene

The sixties was a decade when British lorry manufacturers could take comfort and pride in the knowledge that the United Kingdom was the biggest exporter of commercial vehicles. Markets around the world clamoured for British engineering, and it wasn't only the Commonwealth countries that demanded lorries bearing the Union flag.

Europe, too, was a major importer of British lorries, examples of which were often seen at work in Belgium, Denmark, Holland and Scandinavia. Rootes and BMC were major players in the export scene, and regularly attended the major European motor shows. Rootes sent its vehicles to Germany, a country which had the potential to increase Rootes' market share throughout

Alvis is a name more associated with military vehicles, which is why the Stalwart was the centre of attention at the 1962 Commercial Motor Show. Able to contend with almost impossible conditions, the amphibious Stalwart did the work of lorry, caterpillar tractor and boat. (Author's collection)

western Europe, and BMC specified export models to satisfy a strong demand. Fodens were used on construction sites in Greece, while ERF received orders from Jordan amongst other markets.

A large consignment of Bedfords was shipped to Africa to work in Sudan's sugar industry, and to Asia for duty in the forests of Malaysia. Australia and New Zealand's market share was satisfied by local assembly.

The oil-producing countries sought the expertise of such companies as Atkinson, Scammell and Thornycroft, and it was to those nations that vehicles, huge in size, extraordinarily powerful with their Rolls-Royce or Cummins engines and seldom seen on Britain's roads, were destined. The expertise of the specialist lorry maker was recognised the world over, but it would be only a matter of time before foreign manufacturers would encroach on a market that was once the preserve of the British.

Foden announced its low-line crane chassis in 1964, and for export specified Deutz air-cooled diesel engines. The vehicles depicted were fitted with both road and crane drive, and had engines designed to work in ambient temperatures ranging from -40°F to +40°F. (Author's collection)

his Mighty Fleet of A.E.C. Vehicles were all fitted with Pilot Hydraulic Tipping Gear

Bodywork to standard or individual requirements can be supplied in Alloy, Steel or Wood

ad Office & Works : Pilot Works Limited, Manchester Road, Bolton, Lancs. Telephone : 5545   London Office : Pilot Works Limited, 3 Southampton Place, London, W.C.1.   Telephone : Chancery 5130

Wimpey is recognised for its mammoth road building and quarrying projects. The firm's fleet of massive AEC dumper trucks,
fitted with Pilot bodywork and tipping gear, is the subject of this publicity item.
(Courtesy AEC/Pilot/author's collection)

Pool of London –
Monday morning –

Giant transformer — India waiting — Scotland
Friday — Newcastle Saturday — Stafford
Sunday — shipment to-day — tight schedule —
no time for breakdowns — dependability vital
— Lucas batteries naturally.

LUCAS
HEAVY DUTY BATTERIES

C.V. SHOW
STAND No. 233

JOSEPH LUCAS LTD · BIRMINGHAM 19

The export scene is graphically illustrated in this evocative piece of early sixties advertising on behalf of Lucas Heavy Duty Batteries. It depicts a Scottish-built transformer being delivered to the Pool of London for embarkation on an India-bound vessel. (Author's collection)

Leyland's six-wheeler Super Hippo with a 17ft 9in (541cm) wheelbase was mainly for export, and powered by a 9.8-litre six-cylinder diesel engine developing 125bhp and coupled to a five-speed gearbox. Tractor units were fitted with auxiliary step up/down gearboxes with a 1.328:1 ratio. (Author's collection)

The oil industry was a market in which a number of firms prospered by supplying vehicles and equipment. One such company was Reynolds Boughton of Amersham Common, in Buckinghamshire, which provided specialised bodies, chassis conversions and winch mechanisms. Shown here is a Bedford Boughton 6x6 conversion with twin boom recovery and front-mounted winches.
(Author's collection)

Shell Petroleum employed Thornycroft Mighty Antars for oil-field development. According to the specification, such vehicles were fitted with Rolls-Royce six- or eight-cylinder in-line diesel engines developing 300 and 333bhp respectively. (Courtesy Thornycroft/author's collection)

(Left) Atkinson specialised in producing vehicles for use in some of the most hostile regions of the world, the type of vehicle seen here being utilised for oil field exploration. Tractor units with 100-ton payloads were usually fitted with Cummins or Rolls-Royce engines. (Courtesy Atkinson publicity item/author's collection)

(Below) Intended for tropical and sub-tropical applications, this Atkinson is designed to have 250hp Cummins or Rolls-Royce engines, and is pictured in service in South Africa. Such vehicles were fitted with five- or six-speed constant mesh gearboxes with auxiliary step up or down. (Courtesy Atkinson publicity item/author's collection)

Foden's export activities involved supplying vehicles to a wide range of customers, including the construction and petroleum industries. Of world repute was Foden's brass band, which is seen here gathered in front of vehicles sold overseas. Dumper trucks were sent to Greece, Guyana, South Africa, Nigeria, India and Australia. (Courtesy Foden/author's collection)

(Left) Greece was one of Foden's most lucrative markets, its dumper trucks seen with the Parthenon behind and the Acropolis in the distance. Foden's steam wagon Britannia is significant because it was being exhibited around the world, arrival in Greece coinciding with a delivery of new dumper trucks. (Courtesy Foden/author's collection)

(Right) Of different design to the dumper trucks seen in the previous picture, this 40-ton gross vehicle was introduced in 1969 and was fitted with a 310bhp Cummins engine, an Allison semi-automatic gearbox with torque converter, and a 32-ton rated rear bogie with double reduction hubs and a hydraulically-mounted half cab. (Courtesy Foden/author's collection)

For the export market, Foden unveiled its 44-ton gross vehicle in the 1960s. Specified with a 275bhp engine, twelve-speed gearbox and 32-ton rear bogie, such vehicles featured the firm's latest ceramic clutch and optional Kysor air-conditioning. (Courtesy Foden/author's collection)

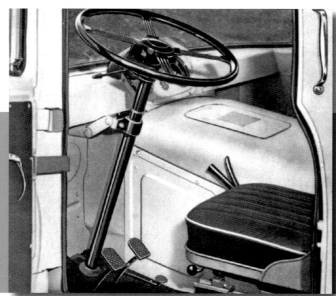

BMC vehicles could be specified with left hand drive and, in this instance, the Morris FF cab. As well as instrumentation calibrated in kilometres, front and rear flashers were standard on all export versions, and special fitment headlights specific to the market were supplied at no extra cost. (Courtesy BMC publicity/author's collection)

Bedford was building thirty trucks an hour at Dunstable in the early sixties, a third of them destined for export. Then Europe's largest truck factory, this 1962 scene shows a TK series cab minus chassis receiving attention. (Courtesy Bedford/author's collection)

Ever ready

Change and development were the key words within the commercial vehicle industry during the 1960s. Amendments to the Construction and Use Regulations had put pressure on the industry with regard to introducing new technology, added to which, competition from European lorry makers provided British producers of lorries with new and demanding challenges.

As if this was not enough, new regulations came into effect late in the second half of the decade concerning vehicles with an unladen weight of three tons and over, and registered before 1st January 1958. These rules required them to be tested and plated at Ministry of Transport Goods Vehicle Testing Stations between October and November 1968.

These were very much behind-the-scenes activities, hidden from those outside the commercial vehicle and haulage industries. Also unseen was the day-to-day maintenance necessary to keep vehicles on the road and delivering to commerce and industry alike.

While lorries were motoring along trunk roads, up and down motorways and negotiating town and city centre streets, not to mention arriving at docks in time to unload wares that were valuable export orders, another industry was frenetically adapting to new technology in respect of vehicle development, building lorry cabs and bodies, carrying out essential repairs, and strapping down cargoes to ensure safe arrival at a destination that was often many hundreds of miles away.

Keeping to schedule in winter often meant enduring bad weather, as this picture shows. Sometimes it was essential to fit tyre chains, but not in this instance when the Atkinson braved blizzard conditions on Easter Sunday 2008. (Author's collection)

Truck tyres have to endure demanding conditions, as is graphically illustrated in this 1962 Firestone advertisement. Tipper trucks are particularly vulnerable to tyre wear owing to the weight they carry over rough terrain. (Author's collection)

Maintenance is essential if a lorry is going to give long and reliable service. The artist of this AC-Delco advertisement has been careful not to identify any particular vehicle, though characteristics of Leyland, BMC and Commer are clearly evident. (Author's collection)

Revised transport regulations permitting heavier payloads during the 1960s encouraged the use of tandem axles on rigid and articulated vehicles. The Holset 'Velvet Ride' suspension, which embodies rubber 'springs' in torsion, is seen here, the manufacturer claiming it to be a technical advance on the 'rubber-in-shear-and-compression' principle. As far as possible, such technology limited jolts and shocks to a lorry's cargo. (Courtesy Holset Engineering)

Work is under way constructing a furniture body, the framework is in place and wooden panelling is being fitted prior to the aluminium sheeting. (Courtesy D. Cook)

(Left) Commercial vehicle coachbuilding is a specialist business, and this photograph shows the construction of a giant furniture lorry at Arlington Body Builders Ltd of Ponders End. The framework has been built in readiness for the sheet aluminium to be applied; in the background a Bedford vehicle is being prepared. (Courtesy P.I.C. Photos)

Specialist coachbuilding sometimes meant acquiring a bare chassis from a manufacturer in order for a bespoke cab and body to be constructed. Such is the case here; the coachbuilder is probably Arlington Bodybuilders Ltd, of High Road, Ponders End, Enfield, Middlesex, which carried out a lot of work on Bedfords as well as Albion and Leyland chassis. (Courtesy D. Cook)

Again probably depicting Arlington coachbuilders, a vehicle body floor is being constructed upon a trolley prior to being transferred to a chassis. (Courtesy D. Cook)

Spray painting is another skill of the specialist coachbuilder. In this instance, the parts of the Foden cab not to be painted have been masked and the technician is applying the paint with a spray gun. Since this photograph was taken, health and safety regulations, as well as paint technology, have changed enormously, which gives this image particular appeal.

The use of synthetic paints provided excellent covering and depth of colour finish with only one or two coats, drying with a high and durable gloss straight from the gun, unlike previous applications, which called for several coats of paint, rubbing down and final polishing. Later developments were the 'half-hour lacquers' that dust-dried in a few minutes, making them ready for service within around thirty minutes. (Courtesy D. Cook)

(Right) This scene shows a Bedford TK under construction at Dunstable in the 1960s. Introduced at the 1960 Commercial Motor Show, the vehicle became a benchmark design which influenced chassis and cab production throughout the British commercial vehicle industry. (Courtesy Bedford)

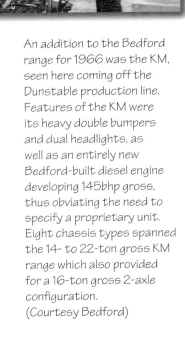

An addition to the Bedford range for 1966 was the KM, seen here coming off the Dunstable production line. Features of the KM were its heavy double bumpers and dual headlights, as well as an entirely new Bedford-built diesel engine developing 145bhp gross, thus obviating the need to specify a proprietary unit. Eight chassis types spanned the 14- to 22-ton gross KM range which also provided for a 16-ton gross 2-axle configuration.
(Courtesy Bedford)

AEC's advertising campaign at the 1964 London Commercial Motor Show centred on its new cab range. This artist's impression depicts the firm's all-round vision tilting cabs, with panoramic windscreen and at-a-glance instrumentation. Cab features were the 7kW heating, saloon car comfort and trim, and engine accessibility. The 'sleeper' version of the cab had a transversely-mounted bunk behind the driver. (Courtesy AEC publicity/author's collection)

Working lorries waiting for the next job may not appear as glamorous as heavily-laden vehicles trundling along an A-road. This BMC K100 truck, pictured in a builder's yard, is typical of vehicles utilised by traders in the 1960s and '70s. (Author's collection)

British Lorries of the 1960s

Another lorry amidst a hardly glamorous scene is this Austin FFK tipper. Such vehicles really were the workhorses of British industry and were rarely in such clean condition as illustrated in this publicity photograph. (Courtesy Austin/BMC publicity/author's collection)

In the 1960s, Carnation Evaporated Milk in distinctive red and white cans was a family favourite (and still is). Wearing Carnation livery is this early sixties Leyland Beaver photographed in the wet summer of 2008. (Author's collection)

More *Those were the days ...* titles from Veloce Publishing –

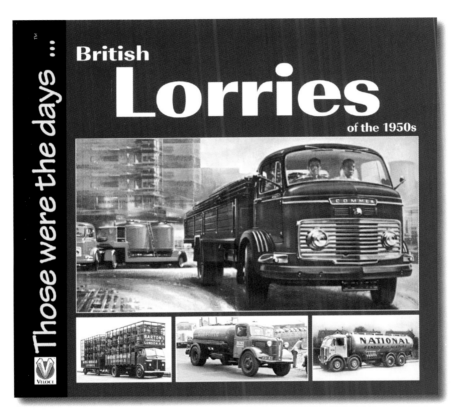

A highly visual look at British lorries produced during the austere 1950s. Familiar and less familiar names connected with the road haulage industry are covered, with comprehensive text revealing much about these productive and essential vehicles.

£14.99
ISBN: 978-1-84584-209-3

For more info on Veloce titles, visit our website at www.veloce.co.uk
email info@veloce.co.uk • tel: +44 (0)1305 260068 • prices subject to change • p+p extra

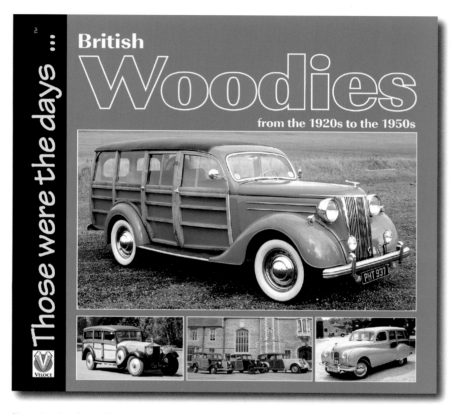

Highlighting the work of hundreds of small coachbuilders, and illustrated with 100 rare and previously unpublished photographs, this book is a tribute to the skills of the people who built these amazing wooden wonders.

£12.99
ISBN: 978-1-84584-169-0

For more info on Veloce titles, visit our website at www.veloce.co.uk
email info@veloce.co.uk • tel: +44 (0)1305 260068 • prices subject to change • p+p extra

More *Those were the days ...* titles from Veloce Publishing –

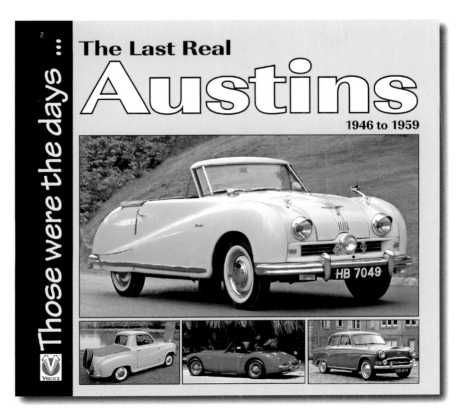

This book examines how Austin bounced back after WWII, and how, despite the severe materials shortage, it managed to develop the largest range of vehicles produced by any automaker in postwar Britain. Illustrated with 100 pictures, many of them archive photographs, depicting the weird, and wonderful – and the downright imaginative.

£14.99
ISBN: 978-1-84584-193-5

For more info on Veloce titles, visit our website at www.veloce.co.uk
email info@veloce.co.uk • tel: +44 (0)1305 260068 • prices subject to change • p+p extra

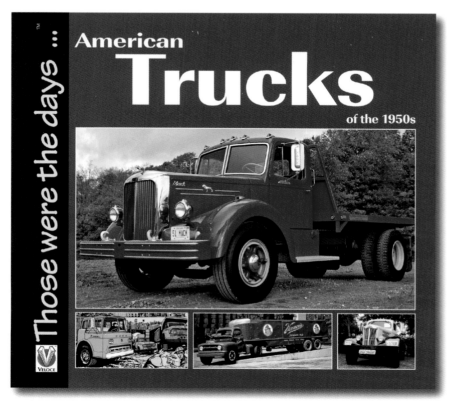

This highly visual study examines the important role of trucks and trucking in the 1950s, recounting the essential role they played in the industrial growth of the US and Canada. Features factory photos, advertisements, original truck brochures and restored examples, plus a comprehensive guide to all models produced.

£14.99
ISBN: 978-1-84584-227-7

For more info on Veloce titles, visit our website at www.veloce.co.uk
email info@veloce.co.uk • tel: +44 (0)1305 260068 • prices subject to change • p+p extra

Index